Contents

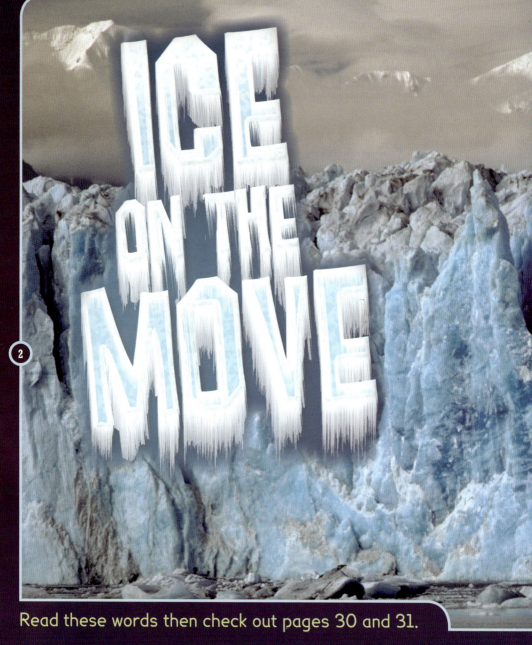

ICE ON THE MOVE

Read these words then check out pages 30 and 31.

arête	cirque	drumlins	esker
uh-RAYT	SERK	DRUHM-linz	ES-kuh

Do you know how a glacier forms? Check out page 5.

Do you know that a glacier moves? Turn to page 6.

Do you know that glaciers change Earth's surface? Learn how on pages 7–11.

Do you know that Earth's glaciers are melting? Find out why on pages 20–25.

Do you know how big glaciers can get? Check out page 26.

fjord	glacial	glacier	moraines
FEE-awrd	grooves	GLAY-see-uh	muh-RAYNZ
	GLAY-see-uhl		
	GROOVZ		

GLACIERS

Written by Susan Mansfield

Do You Know What a Glacier Is?

Think of a lot of ice!
A **glacier** is mostly ice.
Some glaciers are like frozen rivers.
They are called valley glaciers.
Some glaciers are much bigger.
Big glaciers are called ice sheets.

4

A huge ice sheet covers Antarctica.

How Does a Glacier Form?

Cause:
A lot of snow falls over a long time.

Effect:
Layers of snow build up.
The layers get heavy.
The snow gets packed down.
In time, the snow turns to ice.
In time, the ice forms a glacier.

Cross-Section of a Glacier

snowflakes

snowpack

firn

ice

Do You Know That Glaciers Move?

They do.
But so slowly you can't see them moving.

Cause:

As they grow, glaciers get heavy.
A force called gravity pulls them.

Effect:

Glaciers move down slopes.
They move down valleys.
They move down mountainsides.

Gravity makes this valley glacier move.

Do You Know That Glaciers Change Earth's Surface?

They do.

They change the land under them as they move.

They change the land around them as they move.

Glaciers do this in two ways.

They wear away the land.

They leave things behind.

A Valley Glacier

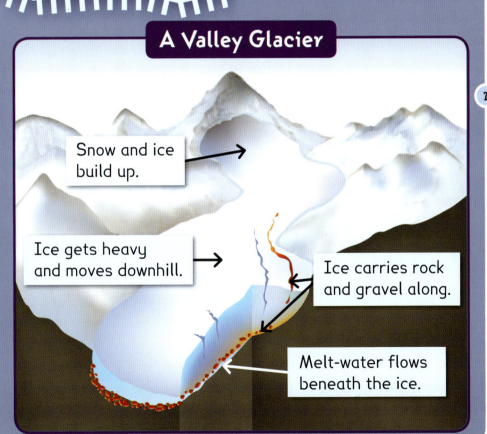

Snow and ice build up.

Ice gets heavy and moves downhill.

Ice carries rock and gravel along.

Melt-water flows beneath the ice.

Cause:
Glaciers wear away, or erode, the land as they move.

Effect:
They make deep valleys by the coast.
Water from the sea fills these valleys.
A sea-filled valley is called a **fjord**.
Fjords are a change to Earth's surface.

Glaciers make sharp mountain ridges.
A sharp ridge like this is called an **arête**.
Arêtes are a change to Earth's surface.

Tricky word
on this page
erode
uh-ROHD

8

A glacier made
this deep fjord.

Glacial grooves in Ohio, United States

The rocks that move in a glacier scratch the layer of rock below. They scratch lines into the rock. These lines are called **glacial grooves**. Glacial grooves are a change to Earth's surface.

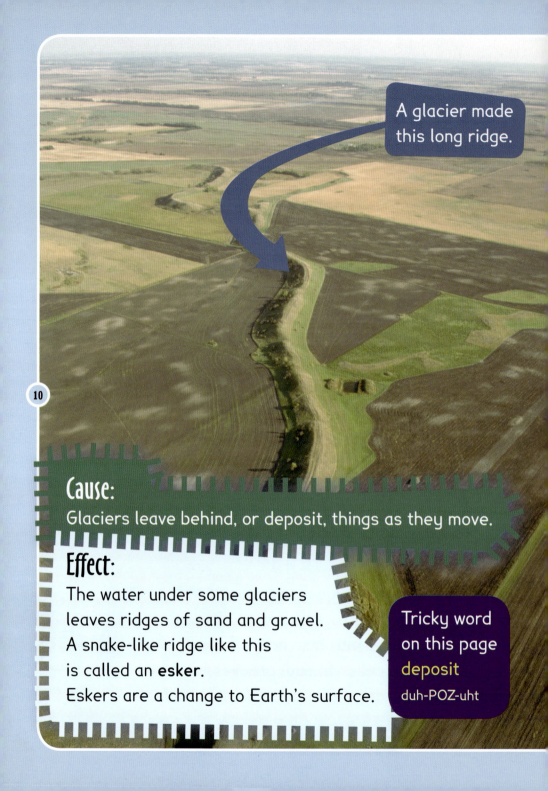

A glacier made this long ridge.

Cause:
Glaciers leave behind, or deposit, things as they move.

Effect:
The water under some glaciers leaves ridges of sand and gravel. A snake-like ridge like this is called an **esker**.
Eskers are a change to Earth's surface.

Tricky word on this page
deposit
duh-POZ-uht

Piles of rock form at the sides of the glacier.
Piles of rock form at the front of the glacier.
The piles of rock are called **moraines**.
Moraines are a change to Earth's surface.

Moraines in Yukon, Canada

Long oval hills form at the base of a glacier.
They are smooth and rounded by ice.
The oval hills are called **drumlins**.
Drumlins are a change to Earth's surface.

What is a cirque? Turn the page to find out. →

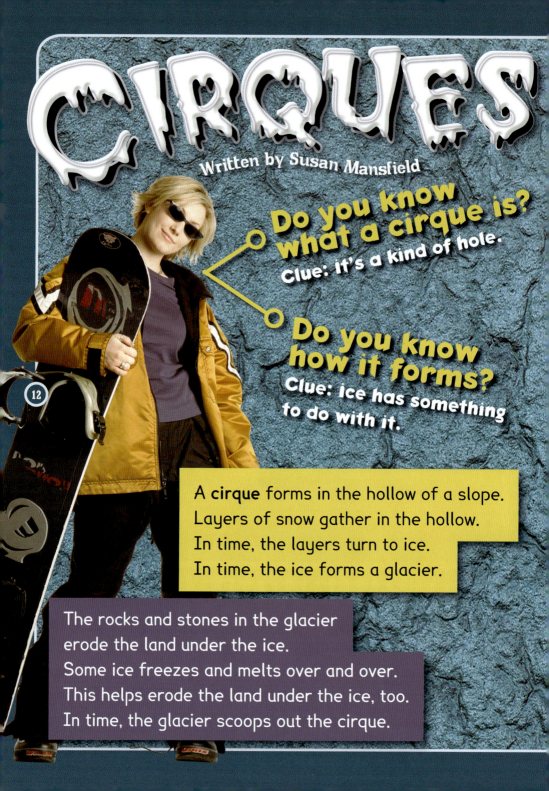

CIRQUES

Written by Susan Mansfield

Do you know what a cirque is?
Clue: It's a kind of hole.

Do you know how it forms?
Clue: Ice has something to do with it.

A **cirque** forms in the hollow of a slope.
Layers of snow gather in the hollow.
In time, the layers turn to ice.
In time, the ice forms a glacier.

The rocks and stones in the glacier
erode the land under the ice.
Some ice freezes and melts over and over.
This helps erode the land under the ice, too.
In time, the glacier scoops out the cirque.

After a long time, the cirque looks like a big bowl.
Sometimes, all the ice in a cirque melts.
The cirque glacier is then a cirque lake.

13

Read on to find out what happens when a glacier adventure goes bad. →

Over the Edge

WRITTEN BY SUSAN MANSFIELD • ILLUSTRATED BY MARK WILSON

High in the mountains, a helicopter drops Emma, Tom, and Jack off to ski a glacier.

Are you sure this is a good idea?

Yeah. We'll be fine. There's a first time for everything.

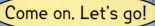

16

Down there. He went outside the markers. Caught a ski on that moraine and flipped over the edge.

I can see him, but he's not moving.

You stay here. I'll ski out and get help.

Hurry, but take care.

I will. I'm not a clown like Tom.

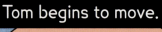
Tom begins to move.

Tom! Are you OK? Can you move?

My legs. I think they may be broken.

Keep still then. Emma's gone to get help.

The ski patrol arrives.

We'll have you out in no time, mate.

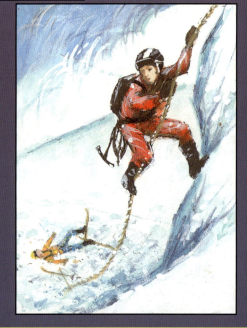

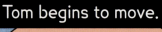

18

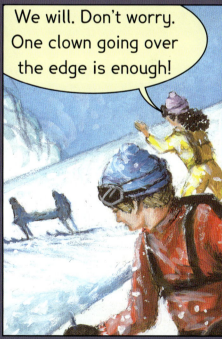

Do you know Earth's glaciers are melting? Turn the page to learn more. →

GLACIERS in Danger

Written by
Susan Mansfield

The glaciers on Earth are melting.
They've been melting for a long time.
They were melting very slowly.
This has changed in the last few years.
Now they are melting much faster.

Penguins on ice
in Antarctica

Do you know why the glaciers are melting?
It's because Earth is getting warmer.

A big layer of gases surrounds Earth.
This layer of gases is called an atmosphere.
The gases wrap around Earth.
They trap heat from the sun.
They help make Earth warm.

Tricky word
on this page
atmosphere
AT-muhs-feer

But now there are too many gases.
They are building up in the atmosphere.
They are holding more heat.
The heat is making Earth warmer.
The heat is making the glaciers melt.

Why are there too many gases?
People have begun to make gases.
They are putting gases in the atmosphere.
Burning fuels can make these gases.
Driving cars can make them.
Clearing land can make them, too.

What will happen if more glaciers melt?
Glaciers store most of Earth's fresh water.
It's normal for glaciers to melt a bit.
The melt-water flows into rivers.
A lot of people get water from these rivers.

They drink water from the rivers.
They use the water to grow crops.
They use it to raise animals.
They use it to make power, too.
What if too many glaciers melt?
In time, there will be a lot less fresh water to use.

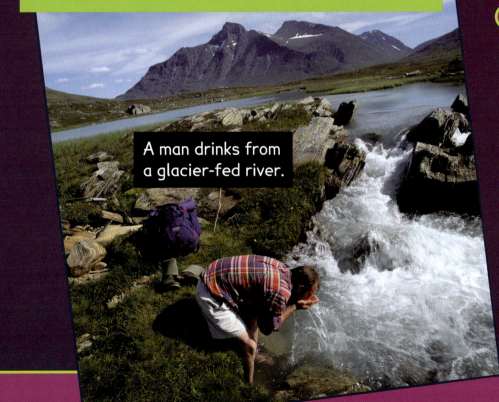

A man drinks from a glacier-fed river.

The melt-water from glaciers flows to the sea.
If more glaciers melt than normal,
the level of the sea could rise.
The sea could cover islands and coasts.
It could wash away land and cause floods.
It could cover low places where people live.

Global warming is melting this glacier.

Do you know what else glaciers do?
Their ice bounces the sun's heat away from Earth.
But if the glaciers melt, less heat will bounce away.
Land and water will soak up more of the sun's heat.
This could make the warming of Earth even worse.

Earth's temperature has always changed.
For a long time, it would be much colder.
Then, for a long time, it would be warmer.
The glaciers grew in the colder times.
Some of them melted in the warmer times.

Some scientists think the new warming is natural.
But most of them think people are to blame.
They say the changes before were slower.
They say that the warming is very fast now.
People know the warming was not this fast before.
They know the glaciers did not melt this fast before.

Multimedia Information

www.readingwinners.com.au

FAQS - - - - - - - - - -

Q How big do glaciers get?

A Some are as long as a football field.
Others are more than 100 kilometres long.
The biggest one is an ice sheet
that covers Antarctica.

Glaciers cover about one-tenth of Earth's surface.

Otzi the Iceman

Otzi the Iceman is a mummy.
His body is over 5,000 years old!

People found his body in a glacier.
The ice made his body stay cold.
It helped stop his body breaking down.

The mummified head of Otzi

This means people could find out a lot about him.
They know that he ate meat and bread.
They know he wore fur and leather clothes.
They even know his body was full of whipworms!
They know he was shot in the back with an arrow.
So how did Otzi die? He died from the arrow wound.
Mummies like Otzi help people learn about life
a long time ago.

Turn the page to check what you have learned. →

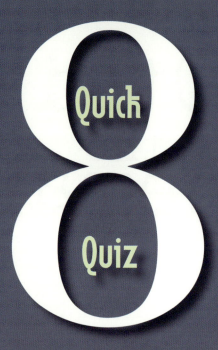

Quick

Quiz

1. What are glaciers mostly made of?

2. What are big glaciers called?

3. How does a glacier form?

4. What two ways do glaciers change Earth's surface?

5. Why are Earth's glaciers melting?

6. Why are there too many gases in the atmosphere?

7. What are people doing to make more gases?

8. How much of Earth is covered by glaciers?

Turn to page 32 for clues. →

Learn More

Choose Your Topic

Choose from this book one landform made by glaciers.

Research Your Topic

Find out more about how glaciers make this landform.
Find some places in the world where the landform is found.

Write Your Article

You may need to make notes first.
You may need to draw maps.
You may need to find photos.
You may need to draw diagrams.
Get your facts in order.
Use subheadings to help you do this.
Write a draft.
Check your spelling.
Check your punctuation.

Present Your Topic

Share your work with other members of your group.

29

arête – a sharp mountain ridge made by glaciers

cirque – a deep hollow in a mountainside made by a glacier

drumlins – smooth, oval hills made by glaciers

esker – a narrow ridge of sand and gravel made by a glacier

fjord – an ocean-filled valley made by a glacier

glacial grooves – the lines scratched into rock by a glacier

glacier – a slow-moving mass of ice

moraines – piles or ridges of rock and sand made by glaciers

Index

Clues to the
Quick 8 Quiz

1. Go to page 4.
2. Go to page 4.
3. Go to page 5.
4. Go to page 7.
5. Go to page 21.
6. Go to page 22.
7. Go to page 22.
8. Go to page 26.